You Have the Right to Retire Happy, Free and Wealthy!

List of Important Decisions that You Need to Make Before Retiring

By: Donna Jackson

9781635014280

I0500168

PUBLISHERS NOTES
Disclaimer – Speedy Publishing LLC

This publication is intended to provide helpful and informative material. It is not intended to diagnose, treat, cure, or prevent any health problem or condition, nor is intended to replace the advice of a physician. No action should be taken solely on the contents of this book. Always consult your physician or qualified health-care professional on any matters regarding your health and before adopting any suggestions in this book or drawing inferences from it.

The author and publisher specifically disclaim all responsibility for any liability, loss or risk, personal or otherwise, which is incurred as a consequence, directly or indirectly, from the use or application of any contents of this book.

Any and all product names referenced within this book are the trademarks of their respective owners. None of these owners have sponsored, authorized, endorsed, or approved this book.

Always read all information provided by the manufacturers' product labels before using their products. The author and publisher are not responsible for claims made by manufacturers.

This book was originally printed before 2014. This is an adapted reprint by Speedy Publishing LLC with newly updated content designed to help readers with much more accurate and timely information and data.

Speedy Publishing LLC

40 E Main Street, Newark, Delaware, 19711

Contact Us: 1-888-248-4521

Website: http://www.speedypublishing.co

REPRINTED Paperback Edition: 9781635014280:

Manufactured in the United States of America

DEDICATION

This book is dedicated to Harry. Thank you for not giving up on me and my dreams.

TABLE OF CONTENTS

CHAPTER 1- HOW RETIREMENT IS PART OF THE AMERICAN DREAM

This is the way the American success story is supposed to go. A youngster gets out of school and finds himself a job in a field of work that appeals to him. He has to start pretty well at the bottom but since Samuel Lucky is a hardworking, intelligent, honest lad, he slowly works his way up the ladder of success. Early in the game he finds Lois, the girl of his dreams and they marry and start up a household. As time goes by the Luckys better their way of life. That is, at first they drove a second hand Chevrolet but after a time they graduate to a new Pontiac. Children come along and they sell their first house and buy a newer and larger one out in the suburbs in a nicer section than they could at first afford.

You Have the Right to Retire Happy, Free and Wealthy!

Most of the neighbors drive Buicks or Oldsmobile and Mrs. Lucky complains that she isn't dressed as well as her friends and the size of their TV screen is smaller than that of the people next door. So Sam Lucky takes to bringing home work from the office in the evenings and working late into the night, and Lois gets a job as secretary in the office of the local clinic. The children are left at a nursery school part of the day. Sam continues to bring work home and three times a week he goes to night school where he takes some pretty stiff courses to increase his worth to the firm.

After a while he gets another promotion and a raise and they can afford a new Buick, and that larger TV set, although in order to swing them Mrs. Lucky has to continue her secretarial job. Time goes by and there are more promotions and the Luckys are able to move to a still better neighborhood, complete with Cadillac, a whole flock of super gadgets, and a maid. Lois, of course, can finally quit her job. Still later they acquire a cook and a chauffeur but in order to achieve these Mr. Lucky continues to bring home work at night. His only recreation these days is playing golf which is invariably done with company customers so that Sam can work on sales at the same time he plays. Mrs. Lucky entertains quite a bit these days—mostly the wives of executives of company customers. By now Sam Lucky has an ulcer and Lois is going every week to her psychiatrist. The children are off in finishing and prep schools.

At the age of 65 Mr. Lucky, who is a vice president in the company now, decides to retire. They do and buy a place in Miami Beach, taking the maids, the cook and the chauffeur along with them. Next year, at the age of 66, Sam drops dead of heart failure. He hadn't been having a very good time anyway. After forty-five years of continual work he'd forgotten how to have a good time. That's the way the American success story is supposed to go but doesn't - at least not for the overwhelming majority of us. This is the way life is more apt to be.

A youngster gets out of school and starts looking for a job. Jim Average might have liked to have become a doctor or engineer but it didn't work out that way. For one thing, his people couldn't afford to finance eight years of pre-med and medical school. The first job that opens up for Jim is in a local print shop where they teach him to do job printing. The pay isn't too good but they tell him he's learning a trade. He works in the print shop for a couple of years and the company puts in some new automatic equipment and Jim Average is let go. Not that he particularly cares. He never did like printing anyway. However, he's started going with Sally who works in a bakery so he needs to get another job as soon as possible. You can't get married on unemployment insurance.

The best job he can locate is clerk in a local super-market and he does his best to please a manager he can't get along with at all. He and Sally get married but since it's necessary for her to keep working if they're going to be able to live in a decent apartment and buy a car, they decide against having children. Down through the years Jim has a series of jobs - factory jobs, construction jobs, a job in a shipyard during the war, another print shop job. Once he and Sally even save enough money to open a service station but for one reason or other it doesn't go over and they lose all the money they invested. Once a depression comes along and for long months the family has no work at all. They have to move in with Sally's parents who can't really afford it.

Children come in spite of planning to the contrary and Jim and Sally sit up nights trying to figure out how to make ends meet. Except for when she's carrying a baby, Sally works at full time jobs. It's the only way they can keep going at all. Some years aren't too bad. During the war and the boom that follows, Jim does pretty well. They even make a deposit on a house and buy a bigger, flashier car. They also go into the hole for a TV set, a new refrigerator, and an electric stove. After which they sit around nights some more, worrying about what's going to happen if either of them lose their jobs. At the age of 55 Jim stops being able to find work except such positions as night watchman or elevator operator in one of the rundown buildings in the industrial part of town. And Sally can only occasionally find employment when her health is up to it, doing housework.

At 65 Jim Average gets his Social Security money and they sell their house and move down to Southern California to retire. However, the amount of Social Security money coming in hardly pays for living on the simplest standard. They get by only because one of the children is able to send them a few dollars each month. These may sound bitter, the above accounts, but they aren't far off the beam. In one case you have a success and in the other you have an average life. For my money, neither of them is worth the living. If I had to make a choice I'd probably choose to be Sam Lucky rather than Jim Average, but neither of them has lived a full life. And as far as retirement is concerned, both of them wound up retired at the age of sixty-five in circumstances which neither can enjoy. Actually, it can be a great deal tougher than even the life of Jim Average which we've painted above. At least he reached the age of sixty-five, which a good many people never do, the pace of modern life being what it is. And at least Jim was able to get jobs until he was 55, a good many find themselves on the scrap heap long before this. And I didn't even deal with the fact that while both Jim and Sally were working, trying to make ends meet, their kids were out on the streets probably taking their master's degree in juvenile delinquency. Nor did we mention that in the life of Sam Lucky he had a fine chance of becoming an alcoholic along the way in view of the pressures upon him. Or that Mrs. Lucky, in spite of her psychiatric visits, had a strong chance of winding up in a mental institute under the tensions of her frustrated life.

We haven't dealt, either, with the probability that after the age of thirty or so there was no longer any real love between Sam and Lois nor Jim and Sally. You don't lead the kind of existence they did and still retain the affection with which you started marriage. Never in the history of any nation have there been such a large percentage of a people in mental institutions. Never has there been such a degree of juvenile delinquency. Never have there been so many divorces. Never has there been such insecurity in the hearts of a people, and our suicide rate is second highest in the world. We Americans, as a people, by no means "have it made."

What are Key Decisions to Make Prior to Retirement?

Deciding what kind of lifestyle the individual is looking forward to enjoying, will be a very important factor that decides the retirement planning process.

Questions such as which location would be ideal, at what age would the retirement commence, what type of dwellings would be needed and any other connecting questions that would help make the relevant decisions.

In some countries the government agencies require a certain percentage of the working adult's salary to be deducted for the purpose of providing some income at retirement.

This income should be considered and supplemented with other retirement plans should it prove to be inadequate.

Setting up a 401(k) would also be an advantage as this would provide the significant tax advantages that would make the retirement plan a more attractive option for those intending to put aside substantial amount of money.

You Have the Right to Retire Happy, Free and Wealthy!

Some individual prefer to invest in stocks and bonds as part of their retirement plans. Though the returns on such investments can be quite attractive there is still some level of risks tagged to this type of plan.

However for some the risk is worth taking and they take the precaution to ensure the investment is done in a diverse way.

CHAPTER 2- HOW TO PLAN YOUR RETIREMENT

Comfortable retirement is all about planning. With proper planning processes in place anyone can retire in the same comforts they enjoyed as working adults or at the very least in a somewhat similar fashion.

The following are some of the planning points that can be exercised as early as possible to ensure retirement in the desired fashion:

Saving – this is the most effective and definite way to ensure a comfortable life as a retired person. These saving put aside should be done in a fashion where it cannot be utilized for any other emergencies or purposes.

The amount of money put aside should also take into account the depreciation rate that the said money would eventually incur. The necessary adjustment should be made to ensure its sufficiency.

Retirement is an expensive situation to be in, especially if there is no comprehensive and strong medical coverage for the individual.

Therefore it is equally important to have good medical coverage policies in place to cover the individual well into old age. Starting such policies at a young age will ensure the individual is not required to pay hefty premiums when compared to others who take out a policy later in age.

Most employees and governing bodies are more than willing to assist the individual in starting a suitable retirement plan. Such plans can be serviced through the specific periodic deductions of an individual's salary. For those who are unable to grasp the importance to a retirement plan, these deductions can often seem rather unnecessary and quite high, but upon some closer understanding of the retirement phase of an individual, these periodic deductions will not seem so daunting. For some property investment is one option toward funds put away for retirement. This is not a style of investment that is suitable for the average person, but nonetheless it is a good option to look into if there is a possibility of being able to invest.

Take into Consideration the Element of Diversity in Investing

When it comes to planning your financial retirement diversity really is the key to turning a significant profit. You do not want to have all your eggs in one basket. For this reason it is an excellent idea to have a number of fingers in a number of pies, financially speaking of course, at any given time. There happen to be a lot of interpretations, unfortunately, of what it means to truly diversify your investment portfolio.

There are those who believe that to diversify your portfolio you only need to choose stocks in various sectors rather than focusing on one. This was a huge problem when the Dot Com boom went Dot Bust. Many people learned valuable lessons during this time frame and have taken it a little bit to heart. However, there is nothing to say that we will never again experience a significant stock market crash. If this were to happen and your entire retirement hopes, dreams, and funds rested on the stock market for salvation you would be in deep and shark infested waters financially as a result.

I do not mean to imply that a stock market crash is probable or imminent by any means. The closest we've come as a nation to a stock market crash in recent memory was immediately after 9-11. The good news is that safeguards were put into place years ago to prevent a crash of the scale that we all know as "The Crash". This means that while you may take heavy hits, chances are the market will recover if you are willing and able to wait it out. However, if you are putting yourself in a position to rely solely on stocks you need to take a serious look at your overall investment plan and see where changes can be made.

It goes without saying that no decision in regards to your financial future should be made without first discussing them with your financial advisor. My purpose here is to bring up questions and ideas you might wish to consider or at the very least discuss with your advisor.

My personal preference is to have some money tied up in mutual funds and other money tied up in real estate, which can provide some form of continuous income month after month. I'm not much of a gambler however and have chosen a low risk path to retirement financing and funding. There are those who are far more adventurous than I when it comes to investing in their financial futures. For those of you who are willing to take the risks there are securities as an investment in order to provide a wildly speculative ride. Securities are very risky for investors; particularly those who are novices and even some seasoned investment veterans tend to shy away from this sort of investment. If you do invest in securities, I strongly urge you not to risk your entire investment on them.

Mutual funds provide a little safer bet when it comes to your financial future. Again there are no guarantees but these are much safer bet than securities. The problem with mutual funds for many is that there are so many from which to choose that it is still a difficult decision for beginning investors to make. These decisions are the reason that a good financial advisor is so terribly important when mapping out your financial destiny.

All in one fund are essentially collections of mutual funds. These provide a safe bet for those who wish to find an easy investment possibility that is a fairly safe (if not wildly conservative) to place your money and watch it slowly grow over time. All in one fund do tend to become less aggressive in time. This means that as you age, they will become more conservative in the placement in your money in an effort to best protect it while still growing your money.

By placing a little of your money in many different places, you will see a much greater safety net when it comes to protecting your profits. Discuss your plans with your financial advisor and any concerns that you may have. Chances are they can help clear up any questions or doubts that you may have.

"There are No Absolutes"

When it comes to investing, whether you are putting aside money in order to send your children to college or aggressively saving for your eventual retirement there are many things you should keep in mind when making your investments. Keeping these things in mind will help you take the successes and losses you experience along the way in stride. This is important as we must keep going and investing if we want to build a solid retirement for ourselves or education for our children. If we give up and decide to play it safe we are seriously limiting our potential. You must learn from your mistakes and work hard not to repeat them rather than letting them rule your future investments.

The first and most important rule to remember is that there are no absolutes. There is no absolute right or wrong method of investing just as there is no one right or wrong way to save your money. There are only the methods that you are more or less comfortable with. The good news is that while diversity is the key in building a strong portfolio, there are many options from which to choose in order to keep your portfolio diverse and, more importantly, profitable.

For today's investor there are all kinds of venues to pursue. You have the choice of stocks, bonds, mutual funds, property investing, and many categories of each of these in between. You should seek the services of a financial planner in order to help you get through those areas that are confusing to you or those that make you uncomfortable. If you are still uncomfortable with certain types of investing after speaking with a planner there is no specific reason that you must pursue any one course of investing over another. It is often the wiser course of action but not necessarily the correct course of action for you as you are likely to make mistakes out of nervousness rather than allowing the fund to do their job and make money for you.

You should also never invest in companies, bonds, funds, etc. for any reason other than you feel they will provide a good return on your investment or you really want to support that particular company. Do not be pressured into making an investment decision that you are not comfortable with unless you are having a hard time risking your money at all. In order to get the returns you will need to provide a proper retirement you will need to take some risks. The greater the risks the greater the potential rewards.

Whether or not you realize it, the choices you make when it comes to your investments affect every aspect of your future retirement or your child's education. You cannot afford to risk those important things too terribly long by being paralyzed by your fear. Fear and anxiety are quite common emotions to experience when handling funds that will have such a profound effect on your future and that of your family. This is a time when a financial advisor or planner is an excellent idea as he or she can take over the reins within reason or course, during these times and pick things up and get them moving in the right direction once again.

There will be setbacks along the way when you are investing funds. I do not personally know anyone who has never lost any money in the stock market. I also know that when you lose money even 50 cents can seem like a tragedy if you allow it to. You must see the bigger picture rather than hyper-focusing on one good or bad decision.

CHAPTER 3- IRA VS. 401 (K)

Understanding IRAs

With all the three letter names floating around our society what is one more? Really? It's not like we don't have enough to worry about without adding this burden. However, when it comes to real life, these three letters will have a greater noticeable effect on people than many of the other three letter names that we here on a regular basis such as the CIA, FBI, NSB, ATF, and countless other abbreviations that are hidden behind three little letters. The good news is that an IRA isn't nearly as insidious as its name would imply. This is a useful tool to most Americans who hope to someday retire from their life of work and life out a somewhat comfortable existence.

There are actually many different IRAs, which is the abbreviation for individual retirement account.

A Traditional IRA is the most common. The only requirement for this particular IRA is that you are employed and that you invest no more than 100% of your income or $4,000 per year, whichever is greater up to the age of 49. At the age of 50 your maximum investment is 100% of your income or $5,000 whichever happens to be greater. If you meet the requirements of the IRS to their satisfaction your contributions to your traditional IRA will be tax deductible. As a result, the funds are not taxed while in your IRA account but once the funds are withdrawn they are subject to federal income taxes.

This is not necessarily a bad thing, particularly for those who plan to be in a lower tax bracket when the funds are withdrawn. However, there is a growing number of people who are interested in the benefits that Roth IRAs and similar funds present by paying the taxes now when the rates are known rather than risk an even higher rate of taxation in the future, even in a lower tax bracket. The best advice I can give is to discuss the matter thoroughly with your financial planner and listen to their advice.

This is a case where only you can ultimately decide which decision is best for your needs but he or she can provide valuable guidance. You should also keep in mind that though laws favor non-taxation for Roth contributions that could change between now and the time you are ready to withdraw your funds, which will have you paying double taxes on those funds and is the primary reason that many people elect to stick with Traditional IRAs instead.

There are several distinct disadvantages to the traditional IRA funds. One of those would be the requirements in order to qualify for tax deductions. First of all, if you have the opportunity to invest in another retirement option through your employer you must be below a certain income level in order to qualify for the tax deduction. If you do not meet that qualification all the funds that are deposited into your IRA fund are subject to federal income tax. You will need to seriously discuss your stock buying strategies before determining if this is the best choice for you as those who buy and hold tend to be penalized when it comes to capital gains.

As things are currently, a Roth IRA is often preferable as the money isn't immediately tax deductible but not only is the investment not taxed upon withdrawal but neither are the gains that were earned on the investment. Another serious setback when it comes to the traditional IRA is that you are required to begin receiving payments at age 70.5. As we are seeing more and more people work well beyond the traditional retirement age this are becoming more and more of an issue.

There are advantages and disadvantages to traditional IRAs. It is important that you decide which of these you are prepared to live with and which you would rather live without. These differences will matter a great deal when retirement comes. Take the time to discuss your goals for the future with your financial advisor and see what he or she recommends.

Understanding the 401 (k)

When searching and sifting through copious amounts of confusing and conflicting information concerning financial retirement savings and plans it is quite likely that you have come across the term 401(k). You may have wondered if that was the newest robot in the Star Wars saga but the truth of the matter is that it is a type of retirement savings plans that is designed so that employees and employers alike can contribute to a fund that is set aside for your future retirement.

Many people invest pretax earnings into their 401(k) funds, which they then have the option to invest in mutual funds of many options. You will find these mutual funds in a wide array of choices from money market accounts to very aggressive and risky stock portfolios. If you work for one of the many companies across the country that offers the option of a 401(k) plan you would be literally robbing your future self not to take advantage of this offering.

There are 3 general types of contributions to 401(k) plans: matching contributions, elective contributions, and non-elective contributions.

Matching contributions are very nice from the standpoint of the employee as the employer matches a predetermined amount of the funds invested by the employee towards this fund. Different companies will offer different amounts for their matching contributions. If your company will match up to a certain percentage of what you invest into your 401 (k) you should take them up on their offer. This is money that will benefit you later in life and should not be thrown away without a darn good for doing so.

An elective contribution is money that you invest before taxes are taken out of your salary. This means that you aren't paying income taxes on these funds at today's rate of taxation. Many people believe this is a good plan because the assumption is that you will be in a lower tax bracket upon retirement though there are no guarantees that that will be true. This money is money that you have elected to invest in your 401 (k) plan, rather than bring home in the form of salary, thus the name of elective contribution.

Non-elective contributions are money that employer deposits into your account. In most cases you cannot opt to take this money as cash rather than an investment in your 401 (k) plan.

There are limitations for how much you can invest into your 401 (k) plan on a given year. You should check with the IRS to get the actual numbers as they have changed over time and are likely to continue doing so as the cost of living increases across the country. Once you reach the age of 50 you are allowed to make extra contributions to your plan in order to 'catch up' and better prepare for retirement.

When studying your options for retirement financial planning you should carefully consider taking your employer up on any type of assistance they offer in this endeavor. If they offer to match the funds you invest in your retirement you can bet that money has already been deducted in their calculations of your salary. In other words, they are giving you the money you've earned in a different manner. The good news is that when the time comes to retire you will be able to appreciate every dollar that has been invested along the way.

We could never hope to simply save the money that we will need in order to retire. Even investments are tricky for the vast majority of the population. For this reason, it is a wise investment plan to take advantage of any opportunity to increase your funds by employers matching your contributions. Take the maximum benefit they will match and if you are seriously worried about your financial future more than your current financial situations, invest the maximum allowable amount each year in your 401 (k) plan.

Commonly Committed Mistakes on 401 (k)

Believe it or not there are many mistakes that can be made along the way when it comes to financial retirement savings and investing. Unfortunately a good many of these mistakes center around the 401(k), which can be a tremendous boost to your retirement plans when used properly in order to build your portfolio. The problem is that the mistakes are often the only things we hear when it comes to retirement plans and investing. I suggest begin with the mistakes so that we can move along to better information and advice in the near future.

The first and perhaps largest mistake that people make when it comes to 401 (k) plans is not signing up. Yes you heard that right. What people do not understand is that this is something your employer offers so that you can have some security for your future. It is a manner of saving money for your future that shouldn't be overlooked or taken for granted. Even a bad 401 (k) plan is better than no 401 (k) and with strict regulations those are few and far between. More importantly, if your company offers to match the funds in your 401 (k) plan not taking them up on that offer is literally tossing money in the garbage can.

The next big mistake when it comes to your 401 (k) is risking too little. Rewards come with risk. If you aren't taking any risks with your investment then you are by and large throwing money down the drain. In addition to that, it is nearly impossible to meet your retirement goals without taking some risks, and some hits along the way. This doesn't mean you should be reckless but along the way you are going to need to take some calculated risks in order to receive the bigger payouts that most of us hope for when investing in their retirement funds.

Risking too much. There are many risks involved when investing in the stock market. There are a few that deserve a little more mention than others. First of all, stocks present a fairly large risk, particularly to the uninitiated. While it is true that great rewards are most often the product of great risks you do not want to risk the bulk of your retirement by investing it all in stocks. Another thing you want to avoid doing if at all possible is investing in your company stock. We've seen too many lives destroyed when companies go under taking the financial stability of their employees along with them. Many companies offer incentives to employees for investing in their stock, which may be tempting but I recommend investing as little as possible in your company stock whenever possible as this could lead to problems down the road.

Finally, the worst thing you can do for the health of your 401 (k) is borrow against it. There are so many ways in which this could go wrong and the penalties for this are more than a little prohibitive. They are designed to be that way so that you will use the funds for their intended purpose. If you absolutely have no other option is the only way I would recommend borrowing against your 401 (k) and I would seriously consider selling a kidney before doing that.

When it comes to your financial retirement, 401 (k) mistakes can be far more costly than you may realize. Work to avoid these common mistakes and you should be well on your way to a successful retirement.

Dealing with Multiple Accounts

When working with those planning financial retirement's one question keeps coming up. Should I consolidate all my accounts or keep them separate? Chances are that you have several different types of retirement accounts from different companies you've worked for along the way. This is not necessarily a bad thing but can be frustrating to try and keep track of.

Combining these funds can be a rather tricky endeavor as many of them are designed to only mate with like accounts. For this reason most 401 (k) plans can only be combined with another 401 (k) the same holds true for many other common retirement accounts including a 403 (b). The one type of account that can accept them all and consolidate them together is a rollover IRA.

Having only one account can simply so many aspects of your retirement that most people wonder why on earth they didn't do this from the very beginning. There are many more benefits than mere ease that goes along with consolidating your accounts and eliminating those extraneous accounts. One of which is the fees that are often charged simply for having the account. These fees can add up over the course of several different accounts and consolidating them into one lone account will eliminate the fees of all the others.

One misconception that people have when it comes to rolling over their accounts is that they will lose their investment options. This is especially a misconception when it comes to a 401 (k) program as if you own a particular investment while it is a 401(k) you will still own the same investment when it's within your IRA account.

In other words a rollover IRA account offers the ultimate flexibility when it comes to your financial retirement needs. You can consolidate all your accounts into one, have all the information in one location and still enjoy the freedom that all the different accounts allowed you to experience in your investing. Diversity is a key ingredient when it comes to successful financial investing procedures.

If you are looking for the best when it comes to financial freedom for your retirement investments you should take the first available opportunity to consolidate your investments into a rollover IRA. Of course you should discuss this with your financial advisor first in order to see if there is a better situation for your unique and personal needs however in many cases the convenience factor of this process is far too tempting to overlook unless there is a very big and specific reason for doing so.

In other words consolidation by and large is very much the way to go when it comes to your retirement funds. You do not however want to sacrifice the diversity of your plan in the process. You should keep your actual investments as diverse as possible in order to insure a well-balanced portfolio that is designed to maximize your profit potential while minimizing your risks.

The decision of whether or not to consolidate your many retirement accounts is as personal as your decision to wear brightly colored socks and ties. There is no absolute right or wrong answer and it quite literally comes down to a matter of preference. If you thrive in chaos then by all means keep five or six accounts going at any given time. If you need neat lines and nice rows that balance out in a glance then consolidation might be the very best thing you can do for your retirement fund.

CHAPTER 4- PLANNING FOR THE REST OF YOUR GOLDEN YEARS

We all know that sooner is much better than later when it comes to planning your retirement. The more money you sock away and the longer that money has to grow and work for you, the better the position you are in to enjoy your retirement to its fullest. With this in mind, you need to approach all of your retirement investments as long-term rather than quick turnover investments.

It is often tempting to risk it all for the promise of a high return on your investment but you must remember that with great reward comes great risk and most of the time your security is simply not worth that particular risk. There are several different types of long-term investments that you may find to be reasonable and even attractive investments.

Bonds are a popular long-term investment. These are very much like bank issued CDs with the minor exception that bonds are issued by the government. There are many kinds of bonds and you should research them all before committing to one over another. If you select the right bond you might find that given enough time your bond will double in value over time.

Mutual funds are another popular investment for long-term investors. These are pools of money that are combined in order to invest in stocks, bonds, and other short-term investment ventures including securities. These funds are handled by the fund manager who decides where and how the money will be invested. This leaves you to reap the rewards that his or her experience will bring in for you over time.

Stocks are another popular option for those interested in long-term investing. It should be noted that investing in stocks is much riskier than investing in mutual funds though the payouts when things go well are often much more substantial. If you decide to delve into the realm of stock market investment you should be aware that every transaction costs money, that you need to thoroughly research the ins and outs of this type of investing, and that you are taking a substantial risk with your retirement investment. You should also be absolutely certain that you thoroughly research the companies in which you plan to invest and only invest in companies that are well established and showing strong potential for future growth.

With any major financial decision you should consult your financial advisor for guidance and advice. His or her job is to help you turn your limited investments into as much money as possible in order to secure your future and your retirement. The guidance that a good financial advisor can provide when it comes to long term investing is invaluable and should not be discounted or taken for granted any more than the advice you would receive from a doctor or an attorney.

My favorite type of long-term investment is real estate. While there are those that will argue that the return on this investment is too minimal to save for retirement I would argue that the fact that properly maintained and rented units will pay for them over time making them pure profit when the time comes to sell or simply to maintain a monthly income throughout your retirement. The more rental properties you own the better your financial position and the more options you have when the time comes to sell those properties. Real estate is one field in which fortunes are made and lost on a regular basis. Rental property is the safest bet for most when it comes to long-term investment and the most significant return on investment. There are options that go well beyond buy and hold when it comes to real estate. If this doesn't excite you perhaps rehabbing property or the even more speculative field of pre-construction investing will offer more appeal.

Long-term investments will be the primary fuel for your financial retirement funds and plans. You need to carefully consider the best possible option for your needs and work towards you financial goals.

Calculate How Much You're Getting to Understand How Your Life after Retirement Will Be

A lot of the calculations done should be noted for its projected style and reference base and not really something absolutely concrete and credible. These are informed and intelligent suppositions based of reliable information, and at the very least it is a guideline of what to expect from the investment in future terms.

Simple interest - Calculating annual interest earnings is usually and ideally done on a 5% interest increment. This is the most basic and simple lest calculations which normally do not take into account any other corresponding effects that may occur sometime in the future.

There is also the possibility of calculating the interest by multiplying what is earned within a year, against the total number of years the individual intents to hold the investments for. The intended time frame for the investment will dictate the amount enjoyed at the end of the period stated.

Compound interest – these kinds of investments are calculated in a clearer and more stable way. The annual interest rates are calculated by adding the principal sum to the interest percentage which is them multiplied by the principle investment amount.

In most cases the interest is fairly stable.

At the end of all the different calculation done the individual ideal target amount for the retirement phase in life should be nothing less than 60% of the current income being enjoyed.

If the amount is bumped up to an ideal 80% then the individual is considered to be able to enjoy a very good and comfortable retirement phase indeed.

Other expenses that are also commonly incurred if the retirement phase is well planned for such as travelling, medical and leisure activities that can be rather costly would also have to be taken into account and provided for adequately. Therefore it is important to consider all sources of current income to be tagged as possible sources for future savings.

Calculate Your Projected Spending

Everyday existence cost money and this is no different when an individual is retired. Therefore future expenses should also be calculated when an individual is still in the working phase in life to ensure the retirement phase quality of life is not severely compromised by poor income sources.

Everything has to be taken into account when drawing up a current annual expenses plan. As there are always additional needs, the additional income needed or expected should also be factored into the plan to better facilitate calculations.

Then the next step would be to measure these figures against the Consumer Price Index, as these indexes provide information for the purpose of being able to make assessments.

The index projects the measured increase in the cost of commonly used goods and then the CPI makes the necessary cost of living adjustments for the Social Security.

There are several sites available and experts that can assist in this exercise should the individual need such assistance.

Studying the various estimation tables drawn up at these sites will give the individual some idea of the connections between markets, labor and costs these two elements effect thus also providing an overview of what to expect for the future.

When perusing the "all items" section of the CPI the individual should be able to multiply the numbers given with the current annual expenses already drawn up for the necessary figured that estimate the future costs and expenses frame.

Most of the information provided at these sites are kept well updated and thus giving the individual real time information. This is very helpful when estimations and concessions made will eventually impact the quality of the retirement phase of the individual's life.

These calculations should ideally be done on a yearly basis, to get a better estimation and working frame of figures to assess the needed adjustments that each fiscal year will definitely bring.

Cut Expenses and Save

If an individual is disciplined enough the ideal situation or mindset would be to cut as much as possible spending and expenses budgets to facilitate higher savings possibilities. This of course is by no means easy, and most of the time it fails to materializes in a disciplined fashion, that is consistent over a long period of time.

Having some tools in place to ensure such savings are done in an unwavering and committed fashion will be very beneficial to the individual in the future though it may not always seem so in the present.

Learning how to identify and cut unnecessary expenses may be difficult to do, but with consistent practice there is always a possibility in being able to cultivate the positive action into a beneficial habit.

When such expenses have been identified, and steps are taken to enforce the cutbacks, the said fund should then be directed into a saving plan that cannot be accessed by the individual easily.

This is due to the fact that there is always be some emergency or another that will require the funds to be tapped into thus eventually leaving the amount less than desirable.

Therefore finding a savings plan that is both fairly committing in style and also one that has all the benefits that would ensure the funds put away accumulate the desired projected interests and the likes, should be a top priority.

Identifying the monthly expenses and breaking it down in a very realistic and committed fashion, will help the individual identify some of the expenses that can be eliminated or down sized and yet still keep the individual is relative comfort and enjoyment, during the working phase of the adult life.

This is important so that the individual will not feel resentment of having to be constantly pressured to save for the future, while not being able to enjoy the present.

Include Your Future Health Care When Planning

Most people plan their retirements without actually taking into account the realism of the health care issues that might arise in the phase in life. Medical care is not only very costly but can also be quite a nightmarish affair. Therefore when planning for retirement there should be a very effective and functional medical plan included in the plans.

For most people the most common choice would be to take out an insurance heath plan that will ideally cover such needs during retirement.

However this is not always adequate as many poorly informed individual can attest to. Most people depend on the advice and directions given by agents who supposedly act in the best interest of the individual, but in most cases the fine print on the policies will dictate otherwise.

Therefore it is important to be as well informed as possible on the policy choices before making a commitment to any plan.

Starting with a suitable fidelity investment summary will help to give the individual some helpful guidelines towards calculating the estimates of the retirement costs and determine the percentages suitable to be included for health coverage.

Disability insurance is another option that is also very popular and should be carefully considered for its more obvious benefits. There is no disadvantage to looking into such possibilities even if its percentage of unfolding is rather limited.

Being ready for any health issues, that might arise just before or during retirement, is something that should be considered with a certain amount of urgency tagged to it. It is also wise to consider some form of long term care insurance. This will help to ensure the individual is able to have access to proper and consistent health care that is of a better quality.

These may include after care and 24hour assisted medical help, should any illnesses occur during the retirement stage.

CHAPTER 5- WHY SOCIAL SECURITY FUNDS ARE NOT ENOUGH TO RETIRE ON

Simply put social security is an income to be enjoyed during retirement or any other phase in the adult life where normal working conditions cannot be expected due to illness or certain forms of disabilities. However, ideally social security income should not be the only income to be enjoyed by this section of society. Studies have shown that it is far from being adequate. It usually meant to function as an assisting source of income and it would be a folly to make it the only source of income for the retired individual.

The following are some of the benefits to be enjoyed as a social security benefactor:

A retirement income upon reaching the age of 62 though this may vary in different parts of the country. Such income can be received in the form of monthly payments to help the individual through retirement.

There is also the rather surprising and equally beneficial payment that can be received by the spouse of the social security subscriber even though the spouse has not actively contributed to such a fund.

There is also some form of medical support given to the individual seeking such assistance during the retirement phase of his or her life.

However it should be noted here, that this assistance may not be optimum care nor will it be available instantaneously, unless the individual is in a critical condition where immediate attention is imperative.

There is also the benefit of being able to receive full medical care from the system that is designed to cater to such retirement age needs. This is also usually extended to the spouse who may not have contributed in any way to the social security plan.

There are also allocations made to accommodate any disabled, minor or dependent children even after the death of the social security contributor.

The Problem with Social Security Funding

While there was once a standard age for retirement in this country and people could count on their company pension plans or retirement funds to get them through their twilight years we are finding that people are often living longer than their funds intended and that their quality of life in these years is much better than in decades past. In fact, we are seeing a growing number of retirees that are dedicated to health and good, clean, fun living. This is something almost unprecedented throughout history and yet our retirees are younger in many ways than ever before.

You Have the Right to Retire Happy, Free and Wealthy!

This is where the problem kicks in for most. If you haven't heard, social security, which was meant to secure our golden years is in serious financial trouble. Part of the reason for this is because people are living longer than was intended when this program was invented. For this reason, we are seeing more and more young people taking their financial retirement planning into their own hands-particularly as we are witnessing more and more retirees coming out of retirement in order to put food on their tables because their retirement funds aren't enough to make ends meet.

It's really sad to see those that must return to work in those years where they should be watching their grandchildren playing rather than going into work day after day. If you don't want this to be you then action needs to be taken. You cannot depend on social security for your retirement and chances are that social services will be a long forgotten thing of the past by the time we reach retirement age.

The vast majority of people reading this will never receive the benefit of social security for the purpose of retirement-unless of course serious adjustments are made in the current system. There are simply too many people living much longer than anticipated. At the same time, regardless of how much you've managed to pay into social security over time it is doubtful that anyone could live on the amount of money they would receive in social security benefits even if they had no other significant bills to pay such as house notes, car notes, or insurance on a home or automobile.

Chapter 6- Where to Invest to Reap the Most Upon Retirement

Real Estate

While many fortunes have been made and lost in the real estate business, many people overlook the value of real estate investing when it comes to planning for retirement. There are many great ways that you can let real estate build a nice little nest egg for your retirement and the sooner you begin the process the better.

While there are all kinds of stocks and mutual funds that confuse even the most intelligent among us, real estate is a pretty straightforward business to get into. The problem is that many people feel it is too risky. The truth is that there are many different types of real estate investing that all carry different risk to the buyer. One thing is for sure and that is that with proper care and attention properties tend to gain value over time rather than lose value. If you purchase properties today and properly maintain them, you can not only reap years of rental income while paying the mortgage on these properties but you can also find your retirement home and pay today's prices for it rather than the prices of tomorrow.

When it comes to real estate it is always good to arm yourself with knowledge before taking any steps and you should carefully discuss all plans for your financial future with your trusted financial planner or advisor. His or her job is to give you guidance when making plans and purchases that will affect your financial stability and security. They can also help you with the matters of taxation, cost analysis, estimated inflation, and the average rise in property value for an area.

As I mentioned before there are always risks when it comes to any sort of investing. The same holds true for real estate investing. Things can go wrong. On occasion you will find lemon properties, for this reason you need to have a complete and thorough inspection performed before you purchase the property. You should also make sure that you are aware of your state and local laws as they apply to landlords. For this reason it is a good idea to consult with an attorney that specializes in this type of financial investing in addition to your financial advisor.

Rental properties aren't the only way to build a property investment portfolio. There are all kinds of property investment opportunities for those that are willing to take the risk. When it comes to property investing, the greater risks often net the greater potential rewards. The thing you must remember is that you are gambling with your financial future. I tend to stick with rental properties as they are a fairly safe bet and actually pay for themselves over the years while building a nice nest egg for my future.

There is the eternally fascinating investment opportunity that property flipping presents for one. When flipping a property you purchase a property below market value-preferably one that requires minor cosmetic repairs. Make the repairs. Then sell the house for a substantial profit. This is a risky venture for those who are novices to the field and many would be investors have lost a great deal of money doing this. Successful investors however can net significant profits in a very short amount of time if they have the knowledge and skills to do the work themselves and time things perfectly.

There are even more property investing opportunities that provide even greater risk, as they are highly speculative known as pre-construction investing. This is the type of investing that creates millionaires. On the flip side it has sent many into bankruptcy along the way as well so tread very carefully before engaging in this sort of real estate investing and take great care never to invest more than you can afford to lose.

As you can see there are ample opportunities in real estate to create an outstanding financial retirement plan for you and your family. The only decision you need to make is whether or not this type of investing is a good fit for your comfort zone.

Stock Market

Stocks provide a very attractive alternative form of investment for those will a little cash in hand. Although there is a certain amount of risks involved in participating in this kind of investment tool the returns are usually quite profitable is the individual is well informed of the background and workings of the company the stocks are based on.

Making informed purchases will limit the liability and losses percentages considerably thus creating a better revenue earning platform that does not require much effort on the part of the investor.

Investing on stock based on hearsay information is not the way to invest in this particular platform as the losses can be considerable. The danger of making an uninformed purchase can be avoided with a little in depth study on the company's portfolio.

Engaging the expertise of those in the field is also encouraged as these individuals are highly trained and knowledgeable in market movements and its corresponding impacts.

There are also several different types on stock investments that and individual can involve in and some of these may include common stock and preferred stocks.

These can then be broken down even further into different classes of stocks which are differentiated by the voting rights the share type holds. This is to ensure the operating power of the company still stays within the intended group.

Buying shares means buying ownership in the company. The ownership ratio would depend largely on the amount of shares bought. The idea behind purchasing such shares is based on the individual's interests and needs to be a participating entity in the said business.

Such shareholders make a conscious choice to play an active role in the daily running of the business entity, which would entail making key decision that will dictate the company future and directions. However such participation would involve a considerable investing capital to procure the intended shares.

Smaller businesses would not need to go through the complicated processes that usually involve extensive legal ramifications, but instead opt to procure investment on a much smaller scale, such as from family members, friends and other interested investors. These investments are usually kept to a minimum to ensure the actual dictating power will remain largely with the intended original controlling party.

For the bigger companies shares can be offered by approaching business angel investors and venture capital investing firms. These entities are always on the lookout for good investment opportunities but they don't necessarily want to actually get involved in an already successful set up. Therefore just being a shareholder that collects on the profits or dividends in enough an investment decision to make. For the actual business owner this can be a rather ideal arrangement as outside interferences can often cause the connecting elements to the business to become confused, with the implementation of conflicting and varied new inclusions in the business engine.

The advantage of this type of procurement capital style is that there is no need to pay off debts caused by borrowings and instead it is simply the exercise of dividing up the profits according to the shareholder's investing percentages. For some this is considered an easier option compared to the others available in the market.

How are Stocks and Shares Different?

To most people who are not savvy in the investing tools that can provide good sources of income. The stocks and shares are just one and the same. However for those who dabble in these types of investments the differences are only too obvious.

Stocks are primary investment style elements that are commonly paid up in full. As for the acquiring of shares, payments can be either in full or staggered. It would all depend on the agreements drawn up by the owner of the business who is extending the participating platform.

Companies that are incorporated are privy to the share issuing style of investments; however this cannot be extended to those wanting to invest as stocks as stock options cannot be issued under these same circumstances.

Therefore only listed companies with strong portfolios can apply to have their company offer stocks as investment opportunities for interested parties.

Stocks have the convenience of transferable facilities that don't require long waiting periods or periods where legal implications have to be sorted out first. With stocks the transferring methods are clear and quick and can be done in fractional parts.

When it come to the shares style of investment the same cannot be applied as firstly shares cannot the divided below the face value of each share nor can the transactions be done conveniently and often.

The legal implications that the transferring of shares constitutes is not as easy or as convenient as that of stocks which can be done registered or unregistered through a simple delivery method. Shares however have to be always registered and are not transferable by just a simple delivery.

All shares have a serial number which depicts the legality of the document. This however does not apply to stocks which are unnumbered serially or otherwise.

How to Trade

Understanding the term fundamentals, would allow the individual to make the relevant connections to the stock market movements from a more informed view.

Basically the fundamentals of a stock refer to its wholesome merits rather than just basing its value on the pricing movement tagged to the stock itself.

Therefore fundamental analysis is more for the discerning investor, who is interested in investing in stocks that have sound business engines backing them.

These may come from proper assessments and performance valuations which the informed investor will insist of being privy too, before actually making the commitment to invest in the said stocks.

Technical analysis usually does not yield the same amount of interest from serious investors, as the price fluctuations usually don't honestly depict the company's capabilities or merits.

The following are some of the fundamental elements that would contribute to investors making bids on the stock market exchange regularly and with impact:

The cash flow of a company being listed on the stock exchange is usually able to meet the most impressive basic requirements before it can be considered suitable for listing.

Failing to accomplish this minimal requirement will result in the particular stock options listing being rejected.

Impressive returns on assets are also another factor that will ensure the stock attracts the attention of those interested investors. Without these returns well documented and visible the business entity would not be able to have the required fundamental placing that is usually sought by investors.

Good fundamentals would have a solid profit history where the retention of such profits fuel further funding for growth possibilities. Investing in such strong entities will give the investor the confidence needed to make the commitment.

This would also encompass the soundness of the capital management of the company where the maximization of the earning capacity is evident.

Understanding Price Changes

Looking at the stock market as one huge auctioning body may perhaps help to explain the better picture on how and why stock process fluctuate. It is all a matter of want versus availability.

Stocks are commonly traded on the value that is placed on it at any given time. This pricing does not in any way reflect the actual fundamentals of the said company but rather it is dictated by the interest expressed in acquiring such stocks.

Basically the value of the company is reflected in the market capitalization which is dictated to by the stock price being multiplied by the number of shares outstanding. Therefore trading the stocks at a lower value but flooding the market will more stocks to be bought will create the scenario whereby the actual price of the stock reflects the expected growth the investors are looking to for the future.

Share prices on the other hand are in theory supposed to be based on more informed buying trends whereby the fundamentals are carefully studied and then decisions are made on when to buy and sell the said shares. However this is only in theory as there is also the "herd sentiment" where movement in the shares is often dictated to by the masses either pushing the price upwards or downward.

Most serious investors will buy into a share based on the strengths it is portrayed to have as it presents a more stable investing option. However this does not mean that the serious investor does not partake in the buying and selling exercise just as the volatility dictates. It would however means that when there is an opportunity to buy at low prices the investor would take the opportunity to buy more stock in the particular company and then sell when the price goes up to make the "quick" cash to then go back and reinvest when the price drops again.

CHAPTER 7- THE BEST PLACES TO RETIRE?

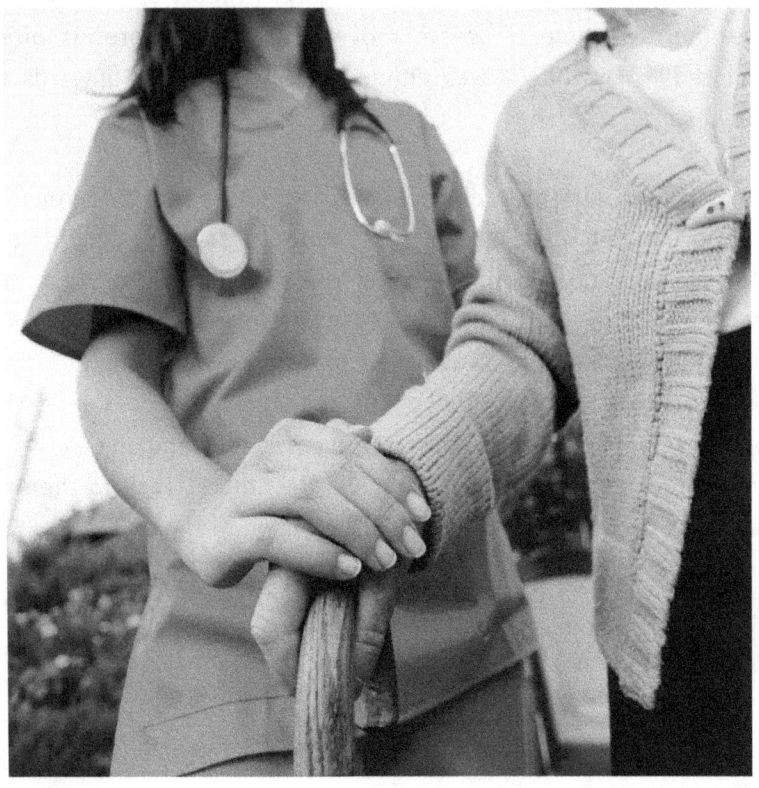

Let's face it. More than four out of every five people living in our country live in unfortunately grim surroundings.

The world is literally full of wonderful, desirable places hi which to reside. But rather than seek them out the overwhelming majority of us live in such traps of humanity as New York City, Chicago, Philadelphia, Detroit, Baltimore, Cleveland, St. Louis, Washington, Boston, Pittsburgh, Milwaukee or Houston. And I've not even mentioned such real holes as Gary, East St. Louis, the coal towns of West Virginia, the textile towns of New England.

And even in our more attractive cities such as Los Angeles, San Francisco, New Orleans and Miami, the majority of the citizenry live in such poor neighborhoods, in such comparative squalor, that the basic attractiveness of the town is lost to them.

It is true enough that even New York or Chicago can be attractive and have their desirable attributes if you have the income of a millionaire but for the average reader of this book such cities mean drab living, too much heat in the summer, too much cold in the winter and sickening carbon monoxide fumes all year round. They also mean high cost of living, even though the living is poor indeed.

Is it hard for you to believe that there are places in the world, even within the boundaries of our own country, where it is possible to live quite well on what rent alone would come to in New York City? We'll come to this and prove it in following pages. Can you conceive of living in a villa on the sea with a full time servant, or possibly even two, all your meals and entertainment paid for, on what it costs to maintain an automobile in Los Angeles? This too we'll prove.

One of the great advantages of being very wealthy is the mobility that becomes yours. Where the average American spends his life in one city, and probably even in one neighborhood, only getting away for quick vacations or occasional business trips of one sort or another, the wealthy are continually on the move. They have both the money and the leisure time to indulge themselves in travel.

Thus a wealthy family can spend their winters in Miami or Palm Beach. But when the Floridian summer is upon them and the heat becomes oppressive, they leave the South and take off for the beauties of New England in the spring. If Old Sol burns too hot, this year, then it's off to Canada on a fishing trip, or up into the mountains for the cooler resorts. If this routine begins to pall, there is always the Caribbean in the winter months, a cruise to Haiti or Trinidad. Or there is Europe with all its resorts, both winter and summer.

It leads to a fuller life, a more complete life, a more educational one. Or, if your family of wealth doesn't particularly like travel but rather wishes to settle down, it can choose the beauty spots of the world, California, Florida, the Southwest, including Arizona, New Mexico and parts of Texas. Often they leave the States completely and establish homes on the French Riviera, the Spanish Costa del Sol, or in Paris, Rome or London if cultural pursuits are of interest.

The point we're leading up to is this. It isn't necessary to be rich to enjoy these things.

Wealth is not needed to travel and certainly not needed to live abroad, or in the most desirable parts of our own country.

It is being done by hundreds of thousands of Americans who have had the determination to get off the treadmill and to lead a full life in retirement from the rat-race. For the amount of money that it costs to buy a new automobile today you could live two or three years in comfort in some of the most beautiful places in the world.

In the body of this book I am going to list a good many of these spots and give detailed information on how much it would cost to get by, or, if you have no income or pension at all, what kind of pleasurable, part time jobs, or small business opportunities are available. However, for right now let me throw a few quick facts at you that might set you back on your heels. That's what we need, so many of us, to be set back on our heels with facts. We need it so that we can be shocked to the point of at last standing up on our feet, showing determination and making a better life for ourselves.

We've all heard of "bargain paradises" where a couple can live for as little as one hundred dollars a month in adequate comfort and even a certain luxury.

They exist! Don't think they don't.

And don't think that what I say is something that applied five years or ten years ago but that in these days of inflation it is no longer so. It is so, now, today!

There are towns, cities, villages and resorts in Mexico, Spain, Austria, Greece, North Africa, Latin America, Portugal and even such exotic places as Turkey, Iraq and the South Sea Islands where living in comfort and even luxury is possible for a pittance.

Did you know that a full time servant will cost you sixty to eighty dollars a month in Southern Spain? That a bottle of champagne in the same country sells for about 60$ in American money?

Did you know that prices are so low in Turkey that you can actually buy a satisfactory three course meal for $10?

That in Mexico it is possible to rent a mansion for as little as $250 a month?

That in such countries as Ireland and England you can buy a tailored Harris or Donegal tweed sport coat for $50 (it would cost at least $250 in the States).

That you can buy a brand new car in several different European countries for less than five thousand dollars? That in tax free Rhodes, one of the most beautiful of the Greek islands, you can buy a German camera cheaper than in Germany, Swiss watches cheaper than in Switzerland, French luxury perfumes cheaper than in France?

Of course, living abroad isn't always suitable, even for we who have decided to make the break and retire from the way of life of the majority to seek happiness, peace and serenity, rather than the carrot on the end of a stick which so many are chasing. If one has children, there is school to be considered. Or there are sometimes other motivations. However, one doesn't have to go abroad to find bargain paradises. Given a correct frame of mind, and a concentration upon the real values you can find them without the bounds of our own land.

I don't suggest that there is anywhere in the United States where you can live on a keeping up-with-the-Joneses basis for a hundred dollars a month. I don't know of any. I do know of many scenically beautiful, climatically wonderful places where life is easy, clothing informal, housing comfortable rather than luxurious and people judged by their real worth rather than the size of their bankroll or car. In such places either on a pension, or at a job or business which doesn't interfere with the good life, you can retire and live at your ease, pursuing whatever it is that really counts in your life, be it hobby, study, art, or just plain fun.

Nor is it necessary to select one spot and take roots there. Remember what I've said about the advantage of the wealthy in having mobility. This might apply to many of our readers, as it once did to me. I spent several years looking over this old world of ours. When I found a delightful spot, I'd settle for a time. It might be in the mountains here, or a river there, on the beach, or in a large cultural center such as Paris. Always I sought the beauty spots, the economical places—and always I found it simple to maintain myself.

Chapter 8- The Different Types of Retirement Plans to Consider

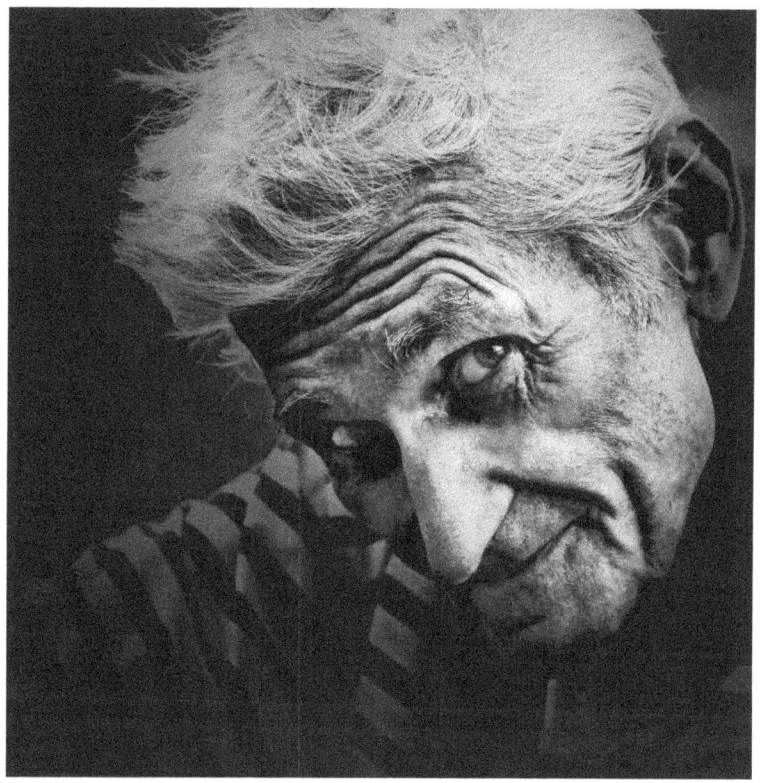

We all know that there is a growing need in this country to take our retirements into our own hands if we want the funds necessary to have any quality of life upon retirement. The problem is that most of us have no idea where to begin when it comes to financial retirement planning or investing. The sad news is that for most of our lives retirement was something that was taken care of if we put in an honest lifetime of work. However, the climate has changed and the retirement funds that many of us have labored to pay for the vast majority of our lives are slipping away.

The good news is that this need has not gone unnoticed by the powers that be and while they aren't offering solutions for the funds we've already invested or in salvaging what is left of the failing system, they are empowering people to take some control for their personal retirements by offering investment options and strategies that provide tax benefits along the way in order to reward you for your efforts.

The four common types of retirement plans include 401(K) plans, Keough Plans, IRAs (individual retirement accounts), and qualifying pension or profit sharing plans offered by corporations. In most retirement plans, the contributions to those plans are tax deductible and taxes aren't paid on these plans until the funds are received and retirement payment begins. You should be careful of your investments and guard them well as there are often hefty penalties involved when you take funds out of your retirement funds before you actually retire.

These of course are not the only types of investments you can make for your golden years and it never hurts to have more eggs in many baskets. The more the merrier in most cases. My personal preference for investing is real estate. This is an investment that you can actually see and reach out and touch. It is also an investment that often gets overlooked when planning for retirement, though when you consider it is an excellent choice. Property values are much lower today than they will be ten, twenty, or fifty years from now. This means the sooner you buy the property the more it will be worth (in theory) when you retire. The thing to remember is that property investing, like other types of investing, requires some degree of risk. You need to learn as much as you can about the process and discuss your interest with a financial advisor before you make any major decisions concerning your retirement investments.

There are more traditional investment methods you may want to consider as well. Mutual funds and the stock market are great ways to invest your money, build a decent portfolio, and increase your net worth. This type of investing also carries some degree of risk and isn't always considered financial retirement planning but more along the lines of simple financial planning.

The thing to remember is that it is always good to have a plan. For this reason, I strongly encourage you to engage the services of a good financial planner. He or she can help you navigate the tricky language that is involved in many transactions, set realistic and obtainable retirement goals according to your needs as well as your means, and offer excellent advice and guidance on other investment ventures you may wish to pursue. In other words, a good financial planner can help you plan for your retirement.

When it comes to the world of finance, many of us are far from experts. We seek legal advice from attorneys, tax advice from accountants, and medical advice from doctors yet very few of us go to financial planners when planning our financial retirement. In many ways it makes little sense to approach our futures so carelessly and yet this is not something that our parents and grandparents would have done so there is no precedence for doing so. The problem is that money is such a limited commodity in this world, we are living longer than ever before, and we are enjoying much more mobility in our golden years than in times long past. We now need expert advice and guidance in order to insure that we are in the best possible position when the time comes to face our own retirements.

Do You Need the Services of a Financial Advisor?

Many people will readily and admittedly seek the services of legal professionals, medical professionals, tax professionals, even domestic professionals but when it comes to financial planning, they rarely seek the assistance of financial professionals. Perhaps it's the result of our grandparent's generation and a fundamental lack of trust when it comes to sharing our financial situation with others. But could it be that this is one area where we are simply afraid to admit that we do not hold the answers? It's money after all; we should be able to control it, where it's going, and what it will do when it gets there right? I'm afraid the answer to that would be, "Not exactly."

Just as the tax codes in this country have become so complicated that you need a magic decoder ring in order to sort through them and actually pay your taxes, so have the rules and regulations when it comes to setting aside funds for the specific purpose of financial retirement planning. One of the reasons they are so complicated is because that many of the plans have very unique and very specific tax benefits either before or after the money is received. In other words, don't put away those magic decoder rings too quickly. You may need them in a few years.

The bottom line is that a good financial planner can help you navigate your way through the treacherous territory of taxes in relation to your financial planning and so much more. Most importantly however, a good financial planner can clue you in to opportunities that you may not know about or may not know enough about. It is their business to know about the many opportunities that exist to set aside and make money for you and your family.

A good financial planner can help you plan for so much more than retirement. In fact, a very good financial planner can help you plan for your retirement, the college funds for your children, emergency funds for life's little mishaps, and a little bit to put towards those special purchases we like to make along the way.

They can do all the things mentioned above by assessing your current situation, your future needs, your current means, and your future goals. They will discuss spending issues that may be problematic, make suggestions, and help you come up with a realistic plan for meeting your goals. Their work doesn't stop there however. They will monitor your progress and when necessary make adjustments that will help you get back on track with your financial planning.

Many people feel that they are perfectly capable of doing this on their own and the truth of the matter is that some people are. The vast majority of us however, lack the discipline, willpower, and the knowledge of investment strategies to make nearly the return on our investments that a good financial planner will yield. When planning your financial retirement and the future of your family you should keep the bottom line in mind at all times. If a good financial planner can net you $100,000 or more in retirement funds over time, he's well worth the price you pay for his service.

Some of the best things about a financial advisor are that you won't have to pay the sometimes high price that comes with learning from your mistakes. You will have his or her knowledge and experience working for your money rather than your own inexperience risking it. He or she can also help you with estate planning and tax guidance so that you aren't left floundering in these matters. He or she can also help you determine your insurance needs in order to protect those you leave behind. There are many ways that a decent financial planner can help you maximize your retirement money the hardest part for you as the consumer is making the call.

CHAPTER 9- IS IT POSSIBLE TO RETIRE WITH A SMALL INCOME?

Give a European a small income, you can almost say no matter how small, and he'll retire, no matter what his age. The average European feels that the most important thing in life is freedom to dispense his time in the way he wishes. He figures that as long as you are at the mercy of a business, even your own, or of an employer, you are not truly free. Others dictate how your time shall be spent.

So you will find throughout Europe and especially in the very economical countries such as Spain, Austria and Greece hundreds of thousands of Europeans, both single persons and families, who have retired at any age from 18 to 80. They simply cannot understand why anyone should continue working after already reaching the point where he, or she, has sufficient funds with which to lead a full life.

I know I am going to run into disbelief here, but I personally have met, in various places throughout the world, single persons, couples and even families who have retired on as little as fifty dollars a month and have no other source of income.

That is correct. Five hundred dollars a month—$6,000 a year.

And when I mention families retiring on that amount, I don't mean per person, I mean the whole family.

Of course, there are a good many more who have retired on larger sums, and any addition at all to this minimum makes considerable difference in living standards, but nevertheless, there are some who stretch out one hundred dollars a month to the point where they can retire on it.

There are hundreds of thousands of Europeans who have re-tired on one hundred dollars a month, or less. In fact, there are few, if any, European nations where the average workingman can look forward to a pension that large upon his retirement at 60 or 65 years of age. Two hundred dollars a month is a fortune in the eyes of the average European. Actually, in most European countries the working man does not make that magnific3nt sum even while employed a full working week. Indeed, there are some European nations, Spain, for example, where even a skilled electrician or plumber, does not make as much as fifty dollars a month, working full time.

However, it would occur to comparatively few American couples who had a guaranteed income of a hundred a month, to retire. Why should this be? That is largely because we, Americans, have established a set of standards which makes five hundred dollars a month hardly more than pin money. There are some who say that this set of standards is a ridiculous one, but ridiculous or not it is there.

If you feel you absolutely must have a new automobile every year or two, then obviously you are not going to be able to retire on a hundred a month—in fact, it'll probably cost you that much to run your car, if you include depreciation and adequate insurance.

If prime quality steak is the only meat that you find digestible, I also doubt that you'll be able to retire on anything like this sum. If your clothes must be the latest styles from Paris, you're sunk and will probably have to keep on that treadmill for a good many more years. If the only beverages you find potable are imported Scotch or cognac, once again it's no go—unless you wish to give up drinking.

It's a matter of sitting down and thinking it out. What is it that you really want in life? What is really important to you?

If you must have the best hi-end gadgets that our civilization has dreamed up, and then you will need a considerable income before you can retire, free of any work, because they are very expensive. In later chapters of this book I am going to illustrate ways in which you can make good money with a minimum of effort, but if you wish to retire completely free of any effort at all and still demand a king-size house, a new car, the most expensive of frozen and canned foods as well as the latest styles in clothing, you're going to have to have a whopper of an income.

However, I repeat, what is really important to you?

More than a million Americans are currently living within the boundaries of our country in trailers. Of these, hundreds of thousands are retired men and women. And of these it has been estimated that more than a hundred thousand have actual cash incomes of less than $6,000 a year. Needless to say, their lives have many advantages. They go where the climate is best, where the scenery is most striking. They fish, they hunt, and they swim when such desires come to them. They see our country in all its glory; they grow to know it intimately.

There is no doubt whatsoever that if you have a sufficient initial amount of money to buy a car (it need not be new) and a trailer (it need be neither new nor large) and an income of approximately one thousand dollars a month, you can retire and see America, Canada and Mexico. Leisurely, thoroughly, happily. There is just no doubt at all. Tens of thousands of other Americans are doing it. You can do it too.

In Miami, to choose only one example among many, there are, thousands of persons who have chosen boats on which to retire, rather than trailers. Hundreds of these boats are docked along the Miami River and in bays and inlets in the vicinity. They range in size from thirty-five feet upward and every type of small craft ever heard of is represented. There are sailboats and motor cruisers, houseboats and yachts.

How much does such a boat cost? You will be hard pressed, perhaps, to believe this, but they run as little as a thousand dollars apiece for boats large enough for a couple to live upon. In fact, the last time I was in Miami I considered buying a several roomed houseboat which was priced at exactly $5,500. I decided against it because it wasn't as mobile as I wanted.

The reason that there are so many craft in the Miami area, so low priced, is due to the nature of our so-called upper class Americans. The usual person, who can afford to buy a boat and operate it as a hobby, wouldn't be seen dead in a model that was several years old. Like their automobiles, they must show themselves off in the very latest. In short, depreciation is very rapid.

A person, couple, or small family, then, can buy these used boats at a comparative pittance. By living upon it full time, rent is saved and many of the playboy-type costs of boating are eliminated. You must pay dockage fees which will run you possibly $200 a month, and if you are on a budget, can't take your craft out on fishing trips or cruises as often as you might like. But even on a tight budget, life on a boat can be pleasant indeed.

Fish becomes a major item in your diet, and, particularly in Southern waters such as Miami, you will find fruits and vegetables in remarkable abundance at low price. If you have never been aboard the type craft of which I speak, I can only tell you that quarters are surprisingly ample, less constricted than a trailer, and the appointments and conveniences of the very best. Only remember that this boat which you have purchased at such a small amount was once a wealthy man's plaything.

But if neither trailer life nor life on the water appeals to you, you might consider one of the cheaper areas of our country in which to retire in a house. It is almost unbelievable, once again, the prices at which you can purchase a small house, or a small farm, here in America.

You see, fifty years ago it was still practical in our country for a family to live on forty acres of land or less and make an adequate living. Every state in the Union had tens of thousands of such small farms. However, as the agricultural revolution developed it became increasingly difficult for the small farmer, with his horse or two, his few cattle, his often-rocky fields, to make a go of it. Every year thousands of farms were given up and their occupants went off to acquire jobs in the city.

In many, many of the beauty spots of America, and I name only New England and the Ozarks of Arkansas, as two examples among the many, these farms remain—for sale at a pittance. You'll find long lists of them in the farm newspapers and magazines. Or, possibly better still; get in touch with the United Farm Agency, 2825 Main Street, Kansas City, Missouri, which specializes in selling farms. They'll send you free catalogues and lists. In the same city is Strout Realty Company, 20 W. Ninth Street, which also specializes in such sales and will also send you free literature on such places.

And not only is the initial investment on these so small, but you'll find that costs of living in general in such areas are far below those to which we are accustomed in the cities. Meats, vegetables, fruits are to be purchased from the neighbors. Chickens and per-haps a pig or two are practical to have in your own backyard. Indeed if amateur farming is of interest to you, such a hobby can pay off nicely.

I am not suggesting if you are city-bred, that you can go out and buy one of these former farms and make a full living upon it by working on a part time basis. It's been done, of course, but on an average you will find that if a farmer, born and raised on a farm, was not able to make a living on this place, neither will you be able to. But you don't have to. With your five hundred dollars a month basic income, you would only be supplementing your diet, picking up a few dollars here and there by selling your surpluses— not attempting to make a full time go of it.

Thus far, I have dealt with retiring in the United States on a minimum amount. And there will be many who have no desire to spend their lives outside the boundaries of our own country.

However, it is my own opinion that a person, or couple, that has a small income, whether it is a pension, or dividends from some investment, can stretch the amount much further by living abroad. As I have already pointed out, a dollar goes much further in such countries as Mexico, Spain, Austria and Greece, among others, than it does in the United States. In fact, the United States is one of the most expensive countries on earth, and many will tell you that it is the most expensive of all.

If you steer clear of the tourist centers, it is possible to live on a very high standard in these countries above mentioned on five hundred dollars a month. Don't forget what I have said above in regard to the Europeans. Very few of them, even in the better to do countries, ever see as much as five hundred dollars a month. Even France, the luxury center of the world, does not have an average income of five hundred dollars a month per family. The average French working man makes less than this by 1997 French government statistics.

It becomes obvious, then, that it is possible to live on this amount. In fact, a bit of consideration shows that since the European is working to acquire his wages, and you are retired, you will have various advantages over him. He must dress for his job; he must utilize the public transportation every day going to and from work. He has expenses you won't have, including taxes, since, as you possibly know, if you live abroad for over 18 months you need not pay American income taxes.

In following chapters we will go into detail on the cheaper countries and the desirable ones in which to retire. It would be duplication to give details here.

Nor will it be necessary to give case histories of Americans who have bought trailers or boats in which to retire. The examples are so many that we all know of them. If not, a short trip to the nearest trailer camp and a bit of conversation, will give you more basic information on the subject than I could list here on many a page. Detailed information on buying a small farm can be found, as I've already mentioned, in the farm publications.

The important thing, the must thing to remember is that the majority of us have false standards. We have been told by the greatest advertising industry the world has ever seen that we have to have this luxury, that we must have that one, that we must spend, spend, SPEND, if we wish to achieve the good life.

Nonsense! The good life is to be achieved by freeing ourselves of this very rat-race which they sponsor. And this can be done on a very small amount, if such an amount is steady and dependable.

CHAPTER 10- KEEP YOUR PRINCIPLES INTACT AS YOU ACQUIRE WEALTH FOR YOUR RETIREMENT

You cannot retire successfully unless you have an assured income or great confidence in securing an adequate income. I want to give you a little lesson in economics—not the kind of economics you might learn in schools or in colleges. In fact, I don't know of any schools and colleges that will teach you this kind of economics. But this is the kind of economics I live by, the kind of economics I have succeeded with. It may be cruel and heartless as many have informed me, but riches are not garnered by soft philosophies and kid gloves.

As a starter you must remember this—keep it in mind always lest you unwarily fall into the wrong hands. All wealth is the end product of labor. Everything that has value is valuable because of human labor embodied in it. All that is useful is not necessarily valuable. For example, water is our most useful product. Yet it is practically free because little labor is necessary to acquire it. On the other side not all things are valuable because labor may be embodied in them. You can go out and spend twenty days with a pen knife and a piece of timber to make a wagon wheel. A great amount of work has been expended but the labor embodied in all this has not been applied to create a socially desirable product. Hence the labor is worthless. Another point! Only efficiently applied labor creates noteworthy wealth. This is to say that labor is expended unnecessarily unless the best and latest production techniques are utilized. Who would think of using lung power to blow bottles and glasses in these days when a machine, itself a magnificent example of embodied human labor of various and manifold types, can make hundreds of thousands of bottles and glasses during the same period of time.

Noteworthy wealth is those products which command a price in the market place. In the long run all products exchange the one for the other at their value. Price is but the monetary reflection of this value, that is, embodied labor. At times price may be above or below the value of a product, depending upon the supply and the demand. But in the long run the price will revolve around a hard core—the value of the product. And labor creates all values! Never be fooled or convinced otherwise on that score. Look again at the most useful thing in the world—water. It is practically free for the taking. Its value is nil. In the deserts it has value and market price— because it requires labor to acquire and bring it to that desert point where it is in demand—where it is needed and wanted. Let us look now at some of our most valuable commodities. Diamonds for example. A diamond cutter may spend days cutting just one diamond. It required quite an expenditure of labor in the first place to mine the diamond. A considerable amount of labor is expended in marketing the diamond. A diamond is tremendously valuable in the market place. Yet it is of less real use than a gallon of water. It is valuable because first it satisfies a human want and is, consequently, in demand as a prized possession. But its real value lies in the labor embodied in its manufacture and distribution. There are many stones that rival its beauty but few so valuable— because they do not represent anywhere near as much embodied labor!

Again I ask you to remember this. Labor is the source of all values! All products are regarded as commodities, bought and sold on the market place at various prices, depending upon the supply and demand. Some are ex-pensive, some are said to be cheap. BUT labor is invariably cheap. It's the biggest bargain under the sun! It can always be bought right! I have bought and sold the labor of hundreds of people in my day! The price I paid was a stipend known by the kindly name of wage—or salary. So I paid $2.50 per hour. Believe me, what I got for that $2.50 was marketable for two to five times that much. That's a markup few finished products will ever stand. That is a markup that labor will almost always stand. The product labor creates usually markets for many times its price, that is, what is paid for it in the form of wages. Perhaps you saw in my literature the mention of wage slavery. I meant that. Let me give you an example.

Back in the early part of the nineteenth century we had an institution in this country known as chattel slavery. Negroes were bought and sold in the market place. They were owned as property just as today we own horses, cattle or sheep. They were owned for only one purpose and that is for the extraction of wealth which their labor created. It was no secret. It was an open affair. A slave was a valuable piece of property. But a slave presented certain problems. He had to be kept in the peak of condition—otherwise he lost his use value and his market value. A sick slave had to be kept and nursed. He couldn't put out the work. If he became crippled it was like throwing $1000 in the fire. He became worthless. The master had to feed and clothe him, shelter him and assure his fitness—just as today cattle and hogs are kept in sleek market condition.

But the Industrial Age reasoned this way. Why should I be Sam's keeper? Why go to all that expense? Pay him a little money instead; let him fend for himself. It's cheaper that way. If I need him he'll be there ready to give out for a stipend. If I don't need him I won't be burdened with him. If the market is slow I won't have to keep him in food, clothing and shelter just the same. I can turn him out. He'll be there waiting till I need him again. He doesn't have any place to go. I get what I want out of him just the same— his ability to labor. And the stipend I pay him is consider-ably less than the expense of maintaining him comes good or bad times. He's not a burdensome worry on me any longer. With this reasoning came about the institution known as the wages system— wage slavery, if you please. It was slavery in another form—a devious form that was not nearly so readily recognized. But slavery it was nevertheless and a form of slavery it remains.

Things are bad, economically, just now. I can put an ad in the Help Wanted columns in tomorrow's newspaper and tomorrow I can have hundreds of applicants knocking on my door, ready and eager to work for me, begging and pleading their consideration over that of competing applicants. Many will accept my terms, my offering wages. "Never mind what you got before. Why don't you go back there? Oh, they just laid you off. Well, if you want to work for me this is it. You don't want to starve do you? Well, I can hire plenty at this wage." And I got my prices all rigged in advance, of course.

Let's say I am a painting contractor—which I assure you I am not—and I get the opportunity to bid on painting a house. I look over the house, figure I can do the job for $550 and come out. I don't worry about my competitors' bids too much. They are like me. If they can't make money on a job—well, what's the use? So we all bid in the same range, maybe I was even a bit higher. So what, I did a real snow job on the home owner. He thought his home would be twice as beautiful with my job as it would have been if anyone else but me painted it. So I got the job. I know it will take about three days for three men to complete the job. This I figure will cost me a total of about 72 labor hours at about $3.00 per hour. I have a $216 labor cost right away. I will need, say, about $120 in paint purchased in wholesale quantities. I figure my wear and tear on equipment and my time and trouble on this job as $100. My overall cost of handling the job will be $436. I make over $100 clear. I might knock out two or three of these jobs a week during the season. I am not working. I am just bidding on the jobs, supervising them and furnishing the precious little equipment needed to get a painting job done. I am the enterpriser knocking down the money. And what is my real secret!

My secret would be simple enough. There are dozens of painters sitting around waiting for a call to go to work. I get calls from some every day wondering if I have any work for them yet. Right here is my secret! I am dealing in the commodity —labor!

What I want to get across to you is this. You can deal in this commodity too! Labor is woefully ignorant. It knows not its value, it realizes little what wealth it creates, and knows little enough about its market price—wages. You can buy it and sell it wholesale. This is one important ingredient that created every great fortune today.

Oh, of course, many acquired great wealth that was not dealing in this wonderful commodity, labor, directly. But they were dealing in the wealth that labor had created, or something that would be valuable only if labor were applied upon it. Again, remember that human labor is the cheapest commodity under the sun! Can you utilize it to your advantage? Can you direct its use in some marketable service or product whereby you reap a bountiful harvest?

I have employed workers as far back as I can remember, here and there, even back in Oklahoma in my teens. When I was a High School boy, it was the custom for a farmer to have the pecan trees thrashed on his place by someone else. It was a dangerous job to climb and thrash trees, especially if you were a farmer well along in years. Pecan harvesting was so hazardous that it was customary to gather the crop for 50% of the harvest. Indians were best suited for this kind of work and could best do it, but what decent Indian would think of work if he were drawing Indian relief? I made arrangements with several farmers in the river bottom areas to thrash their pecans. Some had groves of them; some had only a few trees. Thrashing begins after the first few frosts and lasts well into December, a period covering as much as two months. Some trees yield as much as two to three hundred pounds of pecans and these trees can be mammoth affairs to boot. With pecans at .15 a pound on the market at that time, I did very well. I climbed trees in the evenings after school and hired other school boys to help me. I had boys and girls gathering nuts from under the trees. On some Saturdays a crew of us managed to thrash five or six of these trees and come up with as much as eight hundred to one thousand pounds of pecans, half of which was mine. In those days wages were only $7.00 an hour for men or boys. I paid off my helpers and often managed to come out with $500 or more for a day's work. But tree skinning wasn't to my liking and for a few seasons pecans never bore because of adverse weather conditions during the spring season. I got the wanderlust too, even before I finished High School. Otherwise, I imagine I would still be down there signing up every farmer with a contract to harvest and market his pecans. I had great ambitions about it at that time.

The point to grasp here is that I, by myself, could have done very little in the way of thrashing pecans and gathering pecans. If I had been working for someone else I might have received $7.00 an hour for my labor. But, as it was, I hired others to help me, paid them the 7.00 per hour and made a tremendous profit thereby. In fact, I didn't even remunerate my labor until I had already marketed their product, the pecans. And this can be the case with you too! Why should you pay for labor before you have put much of its product on the market? I am presently an employer. I pay my employees weekly. And I am not paying them for the work they did this week. No sir! They are getting paid for the work they did for me—last week!

A little capital can go a long way. Perhaps you have heard of the contraption known as the cotton picker. They aren't the best machines in the world because they can't hold a torch to a man dragging a cotton sack down a row. That is, from their performance in the field. They leave fully a third of the cotton lying loose on the ground and the cotton gathered is full of leaves, bolls, stems and whatnot. The cotton lying on the ground after a cotton picker is usually picked up on the halves, by Mexicans in the West Texas district of whence I speak now.

A Cotton Picker will gather up to 25 bales of cotton a day with two operators. The best a boll puller can do by hand is around 1000 pounds if he really puts out. The average is around 500 pounds. It requires 2000 pounds of cotton in the boll to make a bale. Can you see the tremendous advantage a Cotton Picker with two operators that gathers up to 25 bales a day has over two boll pullers who between them can gather only 1/2 bale?

I am retired as much as an employer as much as for any other reason and believe me I could be retired for many other reasons than that of my position as an employer. But my reasoning is like this. If I had a business with 20 employees, why should I beat my brains out to keep things in line? I am only one man. If the business is worth having it is worth a good general manager. There are plenty of people around willing to risk a few ulcers for $40,000 to $50,000 a year. So why should I worry? Instead of so much and so much a year I come out with so much less. But so what? I am enjoying myself in the meantime. I am still making plenty of money. I am free to go here and go there. That's the trouble with too many businessmen. They don't own a business. It owns them. Heck, it only takes one man to replace them. That is all it took to replace me in any business that I ever started—just one good man. Every business is, no matter what line you may call it, just a business of dealing in labor, either directly or indirectly.

The acquisition of wealth is not exactly an easy task. If you have a penetrating mind you might turn up more situations than you can hope to cope with. This is my case. In fact, I sometimes find myself spread too thin on a project to project basis. At heart I am lazy and the comment has been made about me that I have worked harder getting out of work than if I had just went ahead and done the work in the first place. But my sort of laziness has developed an imagination that I am proud to brag about. And I can see opportunity in just about anything—perhaps from my varied background and experience—and perhaps because I try to look at it from the viewpoint of "How can I make something out of this and still be down on the creek fishing?" I have heard it said that it was the lazy man who was faced with work that invented a way of getting around it. I have a great love for the wealth and pleasures of this world. I don't intend to let work or duty stand in my way. As long as the commodity—LABOR—is around at such a bargain and is so ignorant why should I involve myself? I can live off the fruits of labor as long as I can utilize it efficiently and competently in the creation of a marketable product or service.

Do you imagine for one minute that the great industrial empires of this day were created by those who own them? If you do just how naive can you get? Is it not just possible that the half million workers whom a giant industrial corporation employs had some-thing to do with the creation of the tremendous wealth the corporation holds title to? Did you know that many corporations have a net worth exceeding the net worth of all their employees combined by as much as 500%? The expression "He went out and made a fortune" isn't exactly true. "He so directed the activity of others that he made a fortune." Labor that works for a mere wage is much like the sheep that gives up its wool for a little food. It gives up just a whole lot more than it gets in return. It is really incredible that the great body of humanity permit themselves to be mulcted so pitifully by a mere handful who owns our industrial wealth. But that is the situation. And with the situation this way why can't you in your little way evolve a little system of your own for dealing in labor to your advantage?

Remember again! To acquire wealth you must somehow lay title to the product of the labor of another. You, yourself, by your own effort, cannot hope to create much wealth beyond your own comfortable needs. The legal way to lay claim to another's labor is to acquire his labor at a price which is considerably less, perhaps only a fraction, of its real market price. When you have mastered the situation to the point where you can employ one kind of labor to manage and corral another kind of labor, then you can free your-self of the whole process, go where you please, when you please, live as you please and enjoy life to its hilt. Others have done it from time immemorial and continue to do it. Why not you, too?

ABOUT THE AUTHOR

Donna Jackson was born in a farm in Florida, where she spent her childhood feeding animals and enjoying sunsets. When she grew up, she became a veterinarian in New York.

Always thinking of the future, Donna saved up for her retirement and is now enjoying the good life at her own farm back home. She is a perfect example of a prepared retiree. Seeing how her retired friends are struggling, she started giving valuable pieces of advice that changed their lives.

Today, Donna is considered an authority on the subject of retirement planning.

www.ingramcontent.com/pod-product-compliance
Lightning Source LLC
Chambersburg PA
CBHW071303170526
45165CB00003B/1403